STEPHEN CURRY

by Elizabeth Raum

AMICUS | AMICUS INK

Amicus High Interest is published by Amicus and Amicus Ink
P.O. Box 1329, Mankato, MN 56002
www.amicuspublishing.us

Library of Congress Cataloging-in-Publication Data
Names: Raum, Elizabeth, author.
Title: Stephen Curry / by Elizabeth Raum.
Description: Mankato, Minnesota : Amicus | Amicus Ink, [2020] | Series:
  Pro Sports Biographies | Audience: Grades: K to Grade 3. | Includes
  webography. | Includes index.
Identifiers: LCCN 2018030402 (print) | LCCN 2018032386
  (ebook) | ISBN 9781681517490 (pdf) | ISBN 9781681516677 (library
  binding) | ISBN 9781681524535 (paperback)
Subjects: LCSH: Curry, Stephen, 1988---Juvenile literature. | Basketball
  players--United States--Biography--Juvenile literature. | African American
  basketball players--United States--Biography--Juvenile literature.
Classification: LCC GV884.C88 (ebook) | LCC GV884.C88 R38 2020 (print) |
  DDC 796.323092 [B]--dc23
LC record available at https://lccn.loc.gov/2018030402

Photo Credits: Alamy/Jason O. Watson cover;
Alamy/Christopher Szagola, Cal Sport Media
2; Alamy/Jane Tyska, Bay Area News Group,
TNS 4, 22; Getty/Brian A. Westerholt 7; Getty/
Vaughn Ridley, Stringer 8–9; Getty/John Leyba
11; Newscom/Kelley L Cox, USA TODAY Sports
12–13; Getty/Jonathan Ferrey 15; AP/ Marcio Jose
Sanchez 16; Getty/Lucas Oleniuk 19; Getty/Thearon
W. Henderson 20

Editors: Wendy Dieker and Alissa Thielges
Designer: Aubrey Harper
Photo Researcher: Holly Young

Printed in the United States of America

HC 10 9 8 7 6 5 4 3 2 1
PB 10 9 8 7 6 5 4 3 2 1

TABLE OF CONTENTS

SUPERSTAR

Stephen Curry **dribbles** the ball up the **court**. He darts left. He darts right. He stops. He shoots. Score! It's a winning basket. Curry is a basketball superstar.

Curry's full name is Wardell Stephen Curry II. He is named after his father.

A WINNING KID

Curry joined his first basketball team at age 6. He's been playing ever since. He went to Davidson College. There, he practiced and played hard. Curry is still the school's top scorer.

GOING PRO

In 2009, Curry joined the pros. He plays for the Golden State Warriors. They are based in Oakland, California. Curry is one of many great players.

One coach calls Curry "Tuna." Tuna fish are hard to catch. They are not big. But they are strong.

LEADER

Curry is the **point guard**. He leads the team. He decides who shoots. Often he makes the shot himself. His baskets help them win.

THREE-POINT HERO

In 2016, Curry made 402 **three-pointers**. No other player had ever made that many in one season. Curry was voted basketball's **MVP** in 2015 and 2016.

Curry has helped the Warriors win three NBA championships.

A FAMILY SPORT

Curry's dad, Dell Curry, was a pro player. He played for the Hornets. His younger brother, Seth, plays pro basketball, too. The brothers learned the game by watching their dad.

Stephen and Seth (right) sometimes play against each other.

FAMILY MAN

Curry is married. He has three kids. The two girls are Riley (pictured) and Ryan. His son, Canon, was born in 2018. Curry's kids sometimes go to home games. When he's away, they video chat.

INSPIRING KIDS

Curry grew up playing basketball. As an NBA player, he helps teach kids the game. He teaches them new skills. He wants them to love playing.

WORK HARD, PLAY HARD

Curry practices every day. He continues to try to be better. He also has fun. "I smile, I laugh, I dance," he says. It helps him be a better player.

JUST THE FACTS

Born: March 14, 1988

Hometown: Akron, Ohio

College: Davidson College

Joined the pros in: 2009

Stats: www.nba.com/players/stephen/curry/201939

Accomplishments:

- NBA Championship winner: 2018, 2017, 2015

- NBA Western Conference All Star Roster: 2018, 2017, 2016, 2015, 2014

- First person to be named NBA Most Valuable Player by unanimous vote: 2016

- NBA Most Valuable Player: 2016, 2015

- Sporting News' College All-American First Team: 2009

WORDS TO KNOW

court – the area where basketball is played

dribble – to move the basketball by bouncing it up and down

MVP – Most Valuable Player; an award given to the player who helped the team the most

point guard – the player who directs the team's shooting action

three-pointer – a basket made from at least 22 feet (6.7 m) away that is worth three points

LEARN MORE

Books
Fishman, Jon M. *Basketball Superstar Stephen Curry*. Minneapolis: Lerner Publications, 2019.

Robinson, Tom. *Today's 12 Hottest NBA Superstars*. Mankato, Minn.: 12-Story Library, 2015.

Schuh, Mari C. *Stephen Curry*. North Mankato, Minn.: Capstone Press, 2016.

Websites
Golden State Warriors | NBA.com
www.nba.com/warriors

Nothing But Nets, supported by Stephen Curry
https://nothingbutnets.net

INDEX

Every effort has been made to ensure that these websites are appropriate for children. However, because of the nature of the Internet, it is impossible to guarantee that these sites will remain active indefinitely or that their contents will not be altered.